FRANKLIN D. ROOSEVELT,
Gallant President

FRANKLIN D. ROOSEVELT,
Gallant President

Barbara Silberdick Feinberg

Lothrop, Lee & Shepard Books
New York

Title-page photograph: President Franklin D. Roosevelt, June 5, 1944.

Unless otherwise noted, all photographs are from the Franklin D. Roosevelt Library, Hyde Park, New York

First Edition
1 2 3 4 5 6 7 8 9 10

Library of Congress Cataloging in Publication Data
Feinberg, Barbara Silberdick.
    Franklin D. Roosevelt, gallant president.
    Includes index.
    SUMMARY: A biography of the man who served as President for more than 12 years, longer than any other man.
    1. Roosevelt, Franklin Delano, Pres. U.S., 1882-1945—Juvenile literature. 2. United States—History—1933-1945—Juvenile literature. 3. Presidents—United States—Juvenile literature. [1. Roosevelt, Franklin Delano, Pres. U.S., 1882-1945. 2. Presidents] I. Title.
E807.F35   973.917'092'4 [B] [92]   80-22307
ISBN 0-688-00433-4   ISBN 0-688-00434-2 (lib. bdg.)

TO MY HUSBAND GERALD,

MY SONS JEREMY AND DOUGLAS,

AND OUR YORKSHIRE TERRIER JENNY

Acknowledgments

This book was written because my sons asked me to tell them about Franklin Delano Roosevelt. As the family project began to appear suitable for publication, a number of people contributed their time, their patience, and their cooperation. I am grateful to the following adults: Regina Cane, Gerald Feinberg, Marjory Rochlin, and Ethel Scheldon who read an early version of this manuscript; Sue Freedman of the Dalton School Library who located some original source material for me; Paul McLaughlin of the Photography Department of the Franklin D. Roosevelt Library who helped me locate and select many of the photographs in this book; and Chaucy Bennetts of Lothrop, Lee & Shepard who taught me a lot about the art of skillful editing.

Several children offered me the benefit of their curiosity, imagination, and opinions. I appreciate the help I received from Randie Cane, James Engel, Douglas and Jeremy Feinberg, and Andrew and Thomas Goldstone.

Contents

FRANKLIN D. ROOSEVELT,
Gallant President

1 A President to Remember

Many American children dream about growing up to become President of the United States and living in the White House. This dream came true for Franklin Delano Roosevelt, who was the thirty-second President of the United States. But for a time, it looked as if the dream could never come true. Franklin Roosevelt had been a healthy, active boy and a vigorous man, but when he was thirty-nine years old he had the crippling disease of polio. It left him handicapped because he could no longer use his legs. He could no longer walk by himself. However, Franklin Roosevelt did not give up. He fought back to lead an active life.

When Franklin Roosevelt became President, America was handicapped also. Too many people did not have jobs, or decent places to live, or enough food to eat. Then came World War II when Americans had to fight to defend their country and its friends. A President who was handicapped helped a nation that was handicapped. The American people elected Franklin Roosevelt to be their President four times. No other President in American history was elected to office more than twice. He clearly had the confidence of the people he led.

Franklin Roosevelt was born on January 30, 1882. The Roosevelt family had come to America in 1620 from Holland. They settled in New York, which was a Dutch colony, and grew in wealth and importance. In time, some Roosevelts came to live at Hyde Park, near the Hudson River, while other Roosevelts lived at Oyster Bay, near Long Island Sound. Roosevelts seemed to love to live near water. Theodore Roosevelt, who was called "Teddy," was an Oyster Bay Roosevelt who became the twenty-sixth President of the United States. Franklin Roosevelt was his distant cousin.

Franklin's father, James Roosevelt, was a Hyde Park Roosevelt who had studied to be a lawyer. He liked to travel, but most of the time he lived quietly at Hyde Park. He was a country gentleman who took care of his land. James Roosevelt had been a widower with a twenty-six-year-old son when he

Franklin as a baby, with his adoring mother in 1882.

married Sara Delano. Sara Delano also came from a rich family. They had made their fortune sailing ships to China and trading goods. Sara Roosevelt was many years younger than her husband. She liked being an important lady. She liked being the wife of James Roosevelt. She was happy when she became the mother of a baby boy named Franklin Roosevelt.

CHILDHOOD AT HYDE PARK

Young Franklin spent most of his time with his mother and his father. His parents gave him lots of love, and he was the favorite of his many aunts and uncles. Early in life, Franklin learned how to get his own way. He did not cry. He did not lose his temper. He learned to be charming and to smile, which usually got him what he wanted. It was a lesson that would help him the rest of his life.

Franklin's parents spent a lot of time with their son. When he was only three, they started taking him with them on their travels. He went to Europe

Franklin perched on his father's shoulder in 1883.

This photograph, taken in 1887, shows Franklin dressed in a Scottish kilt.

with them almost every year. The family spent summer vacations at Campobello Island; it was in the Atlantic Ocean off the coast of New Brunswick, Canada. James Roosevelt had bought the entire island and had a house built on it.

Franklin Roosevelt did not go to school. Like many children of rich parents, he was taught at home by nurses, governesses, and tutors. He had special times for work and special times for play.

This is Franklin on his pony Debby in 1889.

His father gave him a pony named Debby, and he learned to ride as soon as he could sit on the pony. When he was eleven, his father taught him to hunt with a gun. Franklin also learned to skate, to play tennis, and to sail. Often, he sailed on his father's yacht, the *Half Moon*. The captain taught him how to sail, and soon he had his own boat. Also there were lots of trees to climb.

Franklin began to collect things. He became interested in stamps. His uncle, Fred Delano, was a

stamp collector, and he gave Franklin his own collection. Soon uncle and nephew together had stamps
that were world-famous. Young Franklin was also
interested in birds. With his father, he studied all
the birds in the countryside near Hyde Park, and
from his father, he learned all about different kinds
of trees. Like stamps and birds, this was an interest
he would keep for the rest of his life.

Most of the time, Franklin was a very happy boy.
However, sometimes he was lonely. He had a half-

*Franklin steering his father's yacht with the help of a friend
in 1888.*

brother, "Rosy" Roosevelt, but "Rosy" was twenty-eight years older than Franklin. He was too old to be a playmate for the boy. Neighbors' children came to play with Franklin, but he did not have many friends. He had spent so much time with his father and mother that he did not know how to play with children. He could not even get on the Hyde Park baseball team.

Franklin loved his family, but he longed to be independent. He wanted a chance to do some things for himself, but his chance did not come until he was fourteen years old. Then his parents decided to send him away to school. He looked forward to going to Groton, a private school for boys.

TO SCHOOL AT GROTON AND HARVARD

Franklin's mother was not in a hurry to send her son away to school, so Franklin Roosevelt entered Groton two years later than was usual. Since he was a new boy in his class, Franklin felt left out. The other boys already knew each other. Franklin was not very good at sports, and he was not popular with the other boys. He had spent too much time

Franklin Roosevelt's first report card from the Groton School, 1896.

being protected by loving adults to know how to get along with children his own age.

Despite these troubles, Franklin was happy at Groton. He liked taking care of his room, which was very small and bare. He liked being away from home and being independent. Of course, he had to obey the rules of the school. Franklin understood those rules: he had to work hard and to learn. He had to behave himself, and he had to be on time for his classes.

At Groton, Franklin had breakfast at 7:30 in the morning before he went to chapel at 8:15. From 8:30 until lunch, he went to classes. In the afternoons there were more classes, but there was also

As manager of the Groton School baseball team, Franklin (in back row, third from right) is surrounded by the players of the 1899–1900 school year.

time for sports, which Franklin liked. After supper, he went to chapel again. From then until bedtime, Franklin had to study his lessons in a classroom. At bedtime, Franklin and the other boys shook hands with the headmaster and his wife; then they left for their bedrooms to go to sleep.

In school, Franklin and his classmates read many books. They wrote compositions and studied foreign languages. They learned Greek, Latin, and some French and German. They went to classes in mathematics and science. They were taught history, too. However, the most important lesson Groton boys learned was not to be found in their schoolbooks. They learned this lesson from their headmaster. He told them to serve their country. He told them it was their duty to go into government when they were men. It was their duty to help others.

The headmaster's lesson was very different from what Sara Delano Roosevelt had tried to teach her son. She had other ideas about Franklin's future. She wanted him to grow up to be just like his father. After college, she wanted Franklin to go back to Hyde Park and become a country gentleman living quietly among his friends. She thought that work in

During a visit to his mother's family in 1897, Franklin poses as a photographer.

government was not proper for a Roosevelt.

When Franklin entered Harvard University, he began to study politics. He learned more about history, government, and economics. He really enjoyed those classes. He did not agree with his mother's view that politics were "dirty."

Franklin Roosevelt with his parents in 1899.

Franklin was also busy with other things beside his studies. He made a lot of friends at Harvard. He joined clubs and went to many parties. Even though he did not get invited to join all the clubs he wanted to join, he was a popular student. He was chosen to be a cheerleader, and met lots of people.

What Franklin liked best was working for the college newspaper, called *The Crimson*. Because he had worked hard at Groton, Franklin was able to finish his studies at Harvard in three years instead of four. He went back to Harvard for the fourth year anyway because he had been chosen to become president of *The Crimson*. That meant that he could write most of the editorials in the Harvard newspaper. Editori-

Franklin bobsledding with his dogs in 1904.

Franklin Roosevelt as president of the Harvard Crimson, *1904.*

als tell readers what a newspaper believes in. *The Crimson*'s editorials told readers what Franklin thought about things.

While Franklin was at Harvard, his father died. Sara Delano Roosevelt was very lonely. She rented a house near Harvard so she could be closer to her busy

Franklin Roosevelt in 1904 when he was a student at Harvard University.

son. During his last year at Harvard, Franklin decided to go to law school like his father. His mother was pleased. Franklin chose to study law in New York City at Columbia University. He was moving to New York to be near his cousin Eleanor Roosevelt.

FATHER OF A LARGE FAMILY

Eleanor Roosevelt was Theodore Roosevelt's niece and Franklin's distant cousin. Franklin had met

Eleanor when she was fourteen and living with her grandmother after her parents died. Her grandmother took care of her, but Eleanor was a quiet, unhappy girl. Many people thought she was shy. Many others thought she was plain. Franklin did not agree with them. During his last year at Harvard, he decided to marry her.

Eleanor Roosevelt was living in New York. She did all the things young women her age did. She went to parties and dinners and met lots of people. But Eleanor did not spend all of her time with her friends. She worked with children and with families that were poor. She helped people who had just come to the United States and felt strange in their new country. Because she cared, Eleanor taught Franklin to care about what happened to poor people.

Franklin and Eleanor were married on March 17, 1905. Most people thought that Eleanor looked beautiful at her wedding. President Theodore Roosevelt came to the wedding and gave the bride away. People were so thrilled to meet the President of the United States that they almost forgot about

Eleanor Roosevelt in her wedding dress.

Franklin and Eleanor. After a brief wedding trip, the Roosevelts came back to New York City. Franklin went to law school, but he was not going to be a

Franklin and Eleanor Roosevelt as a young married couple, sitting on the porch at Hyde Park in 1906.

lawyer! He had decided to become a politician like his Cousin Teddy.

From 1906 to 1916, Franklin and Eleanor had five children: Anna Eleanor, James, Elliott, Franklin, Jr., and John. Eleanor did not have much chance to take care of her babies. Sara Delano thought they should have nurses and governesses, and Eleanor and Franklin did what she said. As the children grew older, they learned to go to their grandmother Sara when they wanted something and their parents said no. Sara Delano Roosevelt usually gave it to them.

Eleanor did spend a lot of time with her children. Franklin was away so much that when he was home,

A summertime picnic at Campobello with Sara Delano Roosevelt in 1913.

he wanted to have a good time with them; he did not want to punish them or teach them things. To Eleanor fell the job of punishment when the children were naughty. Also Eleanor taught the children. From her, they learned to try new things, to be brave, and to listen and to pay attention.

The Roosevelt family traveled a lot, because

Sara Delano Roosevelt pours tea for Eleanor Roosevelt and Anna on a sailboat at Campobello in 1909.

Franklin was becoming more and more important. They lived in many places—Albany, Hyde Park, New York City, and Washington, D.C. No matter where they were living, they spent summer vacations on the island of Campobello. There the children could swim and sail. They also liked to play baseball. They often went on picnics and romped with their pet dogs and rabbits.

The children particularly enjoyed playing outdoors with their father. He was much better at sports than their mother was, but he was away so much. It was always exciting when he came home. Later in his career, Franklin Roosevelt came to Campobello on Navy warships. How the children looked forward to those times!

2 A Beginner in Politics

Franklin Roosevelt admired his Cousin Teddy so much that he wanted to do the same things Teddy did. He wanted to get into politics. But there was an important difference between the two cousins: Theodore Roosevelt was a Republican and Franklin Roosevelt was a Democrat. Almost everyone elected to political office in the United States belonged to one of the two great political parties, the Republican party or the Democratic party. The only time Franklin ever voted for a Republican was when he voted for Teddy to become President of the United States, in 1904.

In 1910, Franklin had a chance to follow in Teddy Roosevelt's footsteps. To begin in politics he went to the New York State Legislature in Albany. State legislatures make laws for the people living in a state. Franklin ran for election as a state senator. Most people living in or around Hyde Park were Republicans, but Democratic Franklin Roosevelt won easily. In Albany, he worked on laws that would help farmers. He also tried to get New York to take

Assistant Secretary of the Navy Franklin Roosevelt reviews the fleet in 1918 at the end of World War I. Mrs. Roosevelt stands behind him.

better care of its land, trees, and water. Then he became interested in Woodrow Wilson. In 1912, Wilson was trying to become President. Franklin Roosevelt worked hard to help him be elected. He traveled around the United States asking people to vote for Woodrow Wilson. Wilson won!

Because Franklin had worked so hard, President Wilson asked him to come to Washington. In 1913, Franklin Roosevelt became Assistant Secretary of the Navy. Theodore Roosevelt had also been an Assistant Secretary of the Navy. For the next seven years, Franklin worked very hard to make the Navy strong. He visited Navy yards and learned how to get along with labor unions. World War I started in Europe, and Franklin Roosevelt wanted America to be ready to fight. He wanted a strong Navy. When America got into the war, Franklin's Navy was ready. He traveled to Europe to look at America's men and ships. He liked his work.

In 1920 the Democrats chose James Cox to run for President of the United States and Franklin Roosevelt for Vice-President. Theodore Roosevelt had run for Vice-President in 1900 with William Mc-Kinley for President, and had won. But James Cox

In 1919, Assistant Secretary of the Navy Franklin Roosevelt joined President and Mrs. Woodrow Wilson for the voyage home from Europe.

Marching through Cleveland, Ohio, Franklin Roosevelt runs for Vice President in 1920 and urges Americans to vote for James Cox as President.

and Franklin Roosevelt lost the election. Franklin had tried very hard to get Cox elected President. He had traveled all over the United States making speeches telling people to vote for Cox and Roosevelt.

Americans did not want to vote for Democrats in 1920. The Democrats had been in office during World War I, and the American people wanted to forget the war. The Democrats wanted the United States to cooperate with other nations in a League of Nations to keep the peace. The American people did not want to cooperate—they wanted to be left alone. They elected a Republican, Warren G. Harding, to be President.

Franklin Roosevelt moved his family to New York City, where he joined a law firm. He also became a businessman. He was disappointed at losing the election, but he did not give up politics. He did not give up his hope of working in government, but he would have to wait.

AN ACTIVE LIFE DESPITE ILLNESS

During the summer of 1921, the Roosevelt family and their friends went to Campobello Island for a

The Roosevelt family vacationing with their dog Chief. Campobello, 1920.

Franklin and Eleanor Roosevelt in 1920, after a swim at Campobello.

vacation. They went swimming, and they went on their usual picnics. Franklin Roosevelt and his close friend Louis Howe liked to sail and to fish. Also, the two men made plans for Franklin to run for governor of the state of New York. But in August, Franklin Roosevelt became sick. Doctors said he had polio. He was taken by boat and train to a hospital in New York City. By then, he was no longer able to use his legs. In the hospital he did everything he was told, and he tried to stay cheerful and hopeful. Franklin Roosevelt wanted to get better.

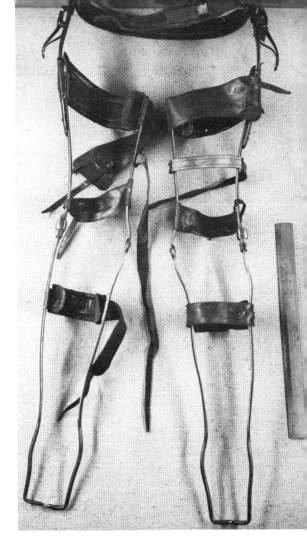

These are the iron braces that helped Franklin Roosevelt to stand and take a few steps by himself.

When he came home from the hospital, he was no longer sick, but he still could not walk. He exercised his legs, but they would not work. He had to sit most of the time in a wheelchair. He had to learn to use crutches. Later, he was fitted with a set of heavy iron braces to put on his legs. They helped him to stand and to walk a few steps. He was still hopeful that someday he would walk again.

To keep busy, Franklin worked on his stamp collection, built model ships, and read many books. He wrote letters to friends and liked to have long talks with visitors. His friend Louis Howe came to stay with him and the family.

His mother, Sara Delano Roosevelt, wanted him to live at Hyde Park. She wanted Franklin to become a country gentleman at last. She had never thought that politics was a proper life for her son. Franklin Roosevelt, his wife Eleanor, and his friend Louis Howe did not agree. Because a man could not use his legs did not mean that he had to spend his days quietly in the countryside. Franklin Roosevelt still wanted to be in government. He just had to prove to people that he could do the jobs that had to be done. He would not give up.

As he began to feel better, he started to travel. He went to New England and to Florida. He felt sad because he could no longer play sports; in particular, he could no longer play golf. However, he found that he still could swim. Swimming helped him because

To get exercise, Franklin Roosevelt joins other polio patients swimming in the pool at Warm Springs, Georgia, in 1930.

in the water his legs were not so heavy and useless. It was a sport he could enjoy even though he had had polio.

In 1924, he learned about Warm Springs, Georgia. He rented a cottage there. He swam in the naturally healthful waters of the Warm Springs pool. It made him feel good because he could exercise his legs. Newspapers wrote about Roosevelt's swimming, and soon other polio patients went to Warm Springs for help. Franklin spent much of his own money to set up a foundation to buy Warm

Springs so that polio patients would have a place where they could swim and exercise. He also built a cottage there for himself. It became one of his favorite vacation places.

Franklin used crutches and braces. Still, standing up and taking steps were very difficult. He could not climb stairs. He learned to get around in his wheelchair, but the wheelchair would not fit into narrow halls. Because it was hard for Franklin to get around, Eleanor Roosevelt learned to take his place. She went to political meetings and began to give speeches. What she saw and did, she reported to her husband. Louis Howe helped her. If Franklin could not go to meetings, at least he would know what was going on.

Franklin Roosevelt began to play an important part in New York Democratic politics again. He had many visitors and wrote many letters to political friends. Democrats asked him to get New York's Governor Alfred E. Smith to run for office once more, and Roosevelt was able to do it. He was even able to get city Democrats and farming Democrats to cooperate.

People across the nation learned that polio had

not kept Franklin Roosevelt from politics. They knew he was back for good when he gave a speech at Madison Square Garden asking Democrats to pick Al Smith to run for President of the United States. Roosevelt could not walk, but he could be a very good politician. In 1928, he worked again to get Al Smith elected. That was a very important year for Franklin Roosevelt—it was the year he became governor of New York State.

GOVERNOR OF NEW YORK

In 1928, Franklin Roosevelt had to make a choice. He could spend all of his time at Warm Springs trying to walk again, or he could try to become governor of the state of New York. Theodore Roosevelt had been governor of New York, and once again Franklin Roosevelt chose to follow in his Cousin Teddy's footsteps. Even though he did have to sit in a wheelchair, he knew he could help the state of New York. He wanted to be in politics, and he could still visit Warm Springs on vacation.

All over the United States in 1928, the Republicans won the elections. Al Smith did not become

President; the Republican Herbert Hoover did. Franklin Roosevelt was one of the few Democrats to win an important office. So when he became governor, people all over America watched what he did. Franklin Roosevelt wanted to do things his own way, and pretty soon Governor Roosevelt did do things his own way.

Roosevelt was still interested in land, water, and trees. As governor, he tried to get his government to use more water power. He wanted the government to give the people of New York more electricity. Water power could make it cheaply. The governor tried to get trees planted on land that was no good for farming. He wanted people to plan the way they used their water and land. He wanted to protect what nature had given to the people of New York.

Governors have to go many places. They have to look at buildings. They have to climb stairs. They have to walk around to see people and things. Since Franklin Roosevelt could not do these things easily, he sent Eleanor out to take his place. She could tell him what she saw; she could help him. That way, Governor Roosevelt knew what was going on in his state. He met with state legislators. Many state legislators were Republicans, but Franklin had been a legislator himself and he knew how to get along with them. Also, he learned to talk to the people of New York on the radio, so he would not have to stand up

With a chair for support, Franklin Roosevelt stands for the ceremony making him Governor of New York State for the second time, in 1930.

Franklin Roosevelt, seated in an open car, is surrounded by friendly crowds in 1932. This was to become a familiar sight.

and make long speeches as often as other governors did.

In 1930, Franklin Roosevelt was elected to be governor again. By 1930, people in the United States were finding that they could not get work so they could not earn money. In New York State, Governor Roosevelt wanted to do something about this. He was the first governor to set up state offices to help people. New York State's government gave people money and created jobs for them planting trees or making the land better for farming. Governor Roosevelt told governors of other states to try this. He told them that government should help people so that they would not have to face troubles all by themselves.

All over the United States, people became more and more interested in Governor Roosevelt. They watched what he did to help the people of his state. They knew that he gave the people of New York good government. They began to think that Franklin D. Roosevelt would make a good President of the United States. In 1932, there would be another election. Meanwhile, the American people were living through difficult times.

3 Americans Suffer the Great Depression

The Great Depression was a time when too many people did not have jobs. It was a time when banks ran out of money, businesses failed, and factories closed down. People had no money for food or clothes, and they waited on long lines to get free food or to get any kind of job they could. People

With all their belongings packed into a car, an Okie family drives West to find work.

couldn't pay their rent, and some lived in tents or shacks made of pieces of wood, tin, and cardboard. These shanty towns were called "Hoovervilles" because Hoover was President when the Great Depression started. Workers, businessmen, teachers, doctors, everybody was having a hard time.

Farmers were in trouble too. People could not afford to buy the food the farmers grew. Without money, farmers could not take good care of their

Free apples, oranges, and rice await this line of hungry people in Cleveland, Ohio.
urtesy of the National Archives, U.S.I.A.

When people lost their homes and savings, they lived in tents and shacks. Such shanty towns came to be called Hoovervilles.

land. To make matters worse, for several years there was not enough rain. Their land turned to dust. Many farmers packed their things into cars and trucks and moved their families out West where they hoped to find jobs. They were called "Okies" and "Arkies" because many of them came from Oklahoma and Arkansas. They were very poor.

Some people marched to Washington, D.C., to ask for help, but Republican President Herbert Hoover sent them home again. President Hoover believed that people should help themselves. He did not want government to give them money or jobs. Instead, he asked people to help each other. But too many people were out of work. Too many people were hungry and cold. The people wanted government to do more for them. They wanted government to help farmers, to control banks, to spend less money, and to find jobs for people.

In 1932, there was an election for President and Congress. The people elected Democrat Franklin Delano Roosevelt to be President of the United States. He had been a good governor of New York State because he understood people's problems and tried to help. The American people gave Franklin Roosevelt seven million more votes than they gave to Herbert Hoover. It was an important victory for Franklin Roosevelt, the Democratic Party, and for the nation.

"THE ONLY THING WE HAVE TO FEAR IS FEAR ITSELF"

When Franklin Delano Roosevelt became President, he told the American people that "the only thing we have to fear is fear itself." He meant that with all the things going wrong in America, the worst was being afraid. Fear made people feel helpless and unable to do anything about their problems. If peo-

At his inauguration in 1933, President Roosevelt tells the American people that the only thing they have to fear is fear itself.

ple could get over being scared, they could act. They could act to help themselves and their country.

President Roosevelt offered them a "New Deal" to make them feel strong and to end the Great Depression. Under the New Deal, the government used many different ways to get Americans back to work again. It tried to help Americans find jobs, it created jobs for people, and it gave them money when there was no work to be had. Slowly, people began to feel good about themselves again.

But times were still hard. Too many people at once had tried to take all of their savings out of banks. They were afraid that the banks would fail and they would lose their money if they left it in. The banks did run out of money and many failed.

To help all Americans, President Roosevelt closed the banks for four days. When the banks reopened, people had some new paper money called Federal Reserve notes. The government promised that if banks ever ran out of money again, the government would pay back Americans who were willing to keep their money in banks once more. That way, people would not lose all of their savings.

To help businessmen who had to close their factories and send their workers away, President Roosevelt asked Congress to pass a law. The law let groups of businessmen and the government set prices for the things people bought. The law protected workers from losing their jobs. The law also made rules for a fair way to sell things. Businessmen who cooperated with the government could put a blue eagle sticker in their store windows and offices. Soon the Supreme Court said that Congress had no right to let the government and business do this. The government had to find other ways to help business.

President Roosevelt helped workers by asking Congress for a law to let workers join unions. Earlier, workers were not allowed to belong to unions unless the unions they joined were run by business. Those unions protected the employers' interests instead of looking after the workers' needs. Under the New Deal, workers got higher pay and shorter working hours. But the New Deal was not able to find jobs for all the seven million Americans who needed them.

To get more money for their crops, farmers had to grow less food. When Congress set up rules to help them do this, the Supreme Court said no. But the government still tried to get farmers to grow less food, to take better care of their land, and to sell extra crops to the government. It paid them to do so. The government gave the food away to people who needed it.

President Roosevelt knew that the people of the Tennessee Valley needed help from their government. He set up the Tennessee Valley Authority, known as the TVA. It built dams so the people of the valley could have electricity, flood control, and good farmland. TVA was a very successful part of the New Deal. It made people's lives better. It gave them lights for their homes, fertilizer for their crops,

Men and machinery building a section of a dam for the Tennessee Valley Authority.

and a safer place to work and play. TVA is a part of the New Deal that is still going on today.

To help young men who were out of work, President Roosevelt set up camps across the country. The young men lived in these camps and worked to plant new trees, to prevent forest fires, and to build roads and bridges. It gave them something important to do. It was healthful to work outdoors, and it helped the country. The government also gave jobs to people to build dams, airports, post offices, and schools that America needed. It even found work for artists, poets, actors, and writers. Franklin Delano Roosevelt's New Deal was the first government program in American history to make work for these Americans. It also gave aid to people who just could not find jobs.

For those too old or too young to work, the President set up Social Security. Under Social Security, everyone who did work and the businesses they worked for paid a special tax. The money from this tax was used to pay people who were poor and most in need of help. That way, when people could not work, they could still have enough money to live on. Like TVA, Social Security is a part of the New Deal that is still going on today. It provides support for people who are temporarily out of work and for those who have retired.

FIRESIDE CHATS

President Roosevelt's New Deal made government bigger. It set up special new government offices called agencies to help the nation recover from the Great Depression. The names of these agencies were long and complicated so people began to call them by their initials, just as they called their President by his, F.D.R. All those initials of agencies, such as AAA, NRA, TVA, and CCC, made the government seem like a big bowl of alphabet soup.

Government also grew because the President asked more people to join the New Deal. To run the new agencies and to give him good advice, F.D.R. asked college teachers, businessmen, writers, and lawyers to help him. So men like Raymond Moley, Bernard Baruch, and Rexford Tugwell came to Washington. These advisers were called the "Brain Trust." In addition, President Roosevelt named the first woman to serve in a President's Cabinet. Her name was Frances Perkins, and she became Secretary of Labor. Along with other members of the Cabinet, it was her job to give the President advice and to see that the President's orders and laws from the Congress were carried out.

President Roosevelt told the American people what he was doing and why he was doing it. He often talked to them on the radio. These talks were known as "fireside chats." The President did not make long, boring speeches. Instead, he talked to the American people from the White House as if he were sitting in their living room chatting with them. That way Americans came to learn about the President's plans. They heard him talk about the laws he wanted Congress to pass. They heard him ask for their cooperation. President Roosevelt's government in Washington did not seem so far away. People

Speaking into radio microphones in 1933, President Roosevelt gives the first of many fireside chats.

could turn on the radio and hear the President's voice tell them what was being done to help them.

The President wanted to know what the people were thinking, too. He read newspapers and got lots of mail at the White House, but that was not enough. The President sent his wife Eleanor and members of his government on trips across the United States to find out how his New Deal was working and how people felt about the government. The people knew that F.D.R. cared what happened to them. They knew that bigger government did not mean that they would feel smaller and more helpless.

ELECTIONS IN 1936 AND AGAIN IN 1940

Since Presidents are elected every four years, in 1936 Franklin Delano Roosevelt ran for President again. He ran against the Republican governor of Kansas, Alfred M. Landon, and beat him by nine million votes! He won in every state except Maine and Vermont. It was a wonderful victory for him and for his New Deal. The American people thanked their President by keeping him in office for another four years.

When so many people voted for him, they showed their confidence in his plans for America. Mr. Roosevelt felt strong enough to try to protect the New Deal from those who did not like it. The President thought that the Supreme Court was the New Deal's biggest enemy. When Congress passed laws the President wanted to help farmers and businessmen, the Supreme Court said the laws were wrong. The Supreme Court said that Congress did not have the power to pass those laws. This made the President angry and disappointed.

After his reelection, President Roosevelt asked Congress to change the Supreme Court. Usually nine men sat on the Supreme Court to judge that American laws were fair and properly made. Mr. Roosevelt proposed that the justices of the court leave their jobs when they became seventy years old. If they refused, Congress was to let the President pick extra judges to join the court. Under Roosevelt's plan, fifteen justices would hear cases if the seventy-year-old justices stayed. Roosevelt felt that with more justices, ones that he picked, the Supreme Court would say that New Deal laws were just what America needed, instead of throwing them out.

The President was not able to change the Supreme Court. Despite his election victory, most Americans did not want a change in this branch of government. However, the Supreme Court soon began to co-operate with the President. For example, it said that Roosevelt's laws to help workers were right. Soon some of the older justices left the court, and President Roosevelt was able to pick new men who agreed with New Deal plans, after all.

While Congress went on passing New Deal laws, the President saw new problems growing. These problems did not have anything to do with the New Deal. There was trouble in Europe and in Asia. President Roosevelt began to think about the threat of war. He wanted to help America's friends in Europe and Asia. He wanted to keep the peace.

By 1940, President Roosevelt's fears of war led him to run for President a third time. No other President in American history had served more than two times. Most Americans thought that there was a rule that no one could be President more than twice, but there was no such rule. President Roosevelt wanted to stay in office to protect his country. He ran for election against Republican Wendell Willkie. He

With his family at Hyde Park in 1940, President Roosevelt waits for news of his reelection.

won by almost five million votes. The American people had shown the President that they trusted him. They trusted him to help them as war drew closer, just as he had helped them in peacetime during the Great Depression.

4 The Arsenal of Democracy

In Europe, Germany was ruled by the Nazi party. Its leader, Adolf Hitler, was a dictator with growing military power. Dictators are rulers who control a country by force. Hitler threatened other nations with war if they did not give some of their land to Germany. In Italy, Fascist dictator Benito Mussolini was making some of the same threats. In 1939, Germany and Italy declared war on Poland. The war spread to all of Europe until only England was left to defend itself alone. In Asia, the Japanese were fighting the Chinese. Germany, Italy, and Japan became partners. They were called the Axis powers.

Fighting in World War I had made the American people and their leaders realize how important it was to avoid another war. They wanted to stay out of troubles in Europe and Asia. Congress passed laws called the "Neutrality Acts" to keep Americans from getting into other people's fights. However, President Roosevelt knew that sooner or later the United States would have to take sides. The Axis powers were capturing all the European countries and taking away their freedom. Meanwhile they could also hurt American trade and sink American ships.

The President asked Congress to change some of the neutrality laws. Congress let England and other friendly nations have goods they needed to make war. Congress said that they would have to pay cash for these things and carry them away in their own ships. Then the President traded fifty old warships to England, and England gave the United States military bases where American men and ships could stay. Finally Congress passed the Lend-Lease law. Under this law, Americans could sell or lend war goods to countries fighting the Axis powers.

These new laws made the United States the "arsenal of democracy." The American government was becoming the supplier of guns, ships, and tanks to countries attacked by Germany, Italy, or Japan. America was not fighting the war, but Americans were helping nations that were at war with the Axis powers.

To make America strong against attack, President Roosevelt asked Congress to require men to serve in a peacetime army. The President also wanted more planes and ships. In his talks to the American people, President Roosevelt explained that England (and later the Soviet Union, too) was fighting America's battles. He warned that the Axis powers wanted to conquer the world. He even let the American Navy and Merchant Marine protect English ships carrying war goods across the Atlantic Ocean. When German submarines began to sink American ships, he gave orders for the sailors to shoot back. While the Americans were busy making their nation stronger and helping the nations fighting the Axis powers, America was still at peace. However, America would not be at peace much longer.

ANGLO-AMERICAN FRIENDSHIP

Alone, England was fighting the Axis powers. England was fighting for democracy against nations that wanted to rule the world. The Americans and the English shared the same ideas about freedom and lawful government. President Roosevelt wanted to help England and her brave people, so he invited the King and Queen of England to visit the United States. He was going to show the Axis powers that the democracies stood together.

In Washington, D.C., the Roosevelts gave a party on the White House lawn and later a state dinner for

In 1939, the Roosevelts entertained England's King and Queen at Hyde Park. Eleanor Roosevelt, King George VI, Sara Delano Roosevelt, Queen Elizabeth, and President Roosevelt pose for photographers.

Wide World p

the royal pair. Then the king and queen visited the Roosevelts at Hyde Park. At home, the Roosevelts gave a picnic for their English guests. Mrs. Roosevelt served them American hot dogs. The President took them around in his special car, a car he could drive himself without having to use his legs.

To discuss the growing threat of Germany's military successes, the President met with England's Prime Minister Winston Churchill in the summer of 1941. The trip was a secret, so the President said he was going fishing for a few days. He left on a fishing boat but was taken to another ship which traveled to meet Churchill. The trip was kept a secret so that the two leaders would not be in danger from German submarines.

Meeting in the North Atlantic Ocean off the coast of Canada, the President and the Prime Minister wrote the Atlantic Charter. The charter told the peoples of the world why the English and the Americans were joined against the Axis powers. It talked about the kind of world England and America wanted to have when the Axis powers were defeated.

The Atlantic Charter said that England and the United States did not want to take other countries' land. They wanted people all over the world to be able to choose their own government. They wanted a peaceful world where men could travel on the seas safely and trade freely. Most of all, they wanted to set up some way that nations could give up wars and weapons. They wanted a way to keep peace.

DAY OF INFAMY

On Sunday, December 7, 1941, most Americans had the day off. All across the nation they were resting, eating lunch, playing, going to church, or doing what most Americans did on Sundays. This Sunday was different because, without warning, Japanese airplanes bombed the American naval base at Pearl Harbor in the Hawaiian Islands. The Japanese also bombed Army airfields and the city of Honolulu.

Most of the American warships in the Pacific Ocean were at Pearl Harbor. This sneak attack sank or badly damaged them, and more than two thou-

In a surprise attack on Pearl Harbor on December 7, 1941, the Japanese destroyed most of the American Pacific fleet.

sand people were killed. Americans were saddened and angry. They realized that they would have to go to war against Japan. Even though most of the Pacific warships had been destroyed, Americans were ready to fight!

Nineteen ships, including eight warships, were sunk or badly damaged at Pearl Harbor. The fires burned for days afterward.

U.S. Navy/National Arch

Elliott

James

John

Franklin, Jr.

Like other parents of servicemen, the Roosevelts treasured photographs of their sons in military uniform.

President Roosevelt went to Congress on December 8. He called the Japanese surprise attack on Pearl Harbor a "day of infamy." What the Japanese had done was so terrible that people would never forget it. It would live on in history as a sad day for America. In answer to the President, Congress declared war on Japan. Three days later Japan's partners, Germany and Italy, declared war on the United States. America was at war with the Axis powers. At last, America had entered World War II.

The President's sons, along with the sons, brothers, and husbands of most Americans, got ready to join the fight. Other Americans went to work building tanks and guns and making airplanes. America needed ships and planes to replace the ones Japan had destroyed. Everyone was united in wanting to win the war against the Axis powers.

The United States was worried that the Japanese who were living in this country might try to help Japan. The government ordered all Japanese-Americans to leave their homes and jobs. They were sent to special camps where they were watched. They could not leave the camps without permission. Life was difficult for them. They were not treated as Americans; they were treated as enemies. Even though they and their families were treated badly by their country, many Japanese-Americans fought bravely in Europe against the armies of Hitler and Mussolini. Strangely enough, the Japanese-Americans who lived in Hawaii were allowed to stay in their homes. They were not forced to live in camps as were Japanese-Americans living on the mainland.

5 Dr. Win-the-War

President Roosevelt told newspapermen that America had had a bad accident at Pearl Harbor. He said that Dr. Win-the-War would help America feel strong again. Dr. New Deal was no longer working on this patient. As Dr. Win-the-War, President Roosevelt traveled all over the world. No other President, even without Roosevelt's handicap, had left his country during wartime.

President Roosevelt had to meet with leaders of other countries at war with the Axis powers. These nations were called the Allies. Their armies had to learn to work together. To get nations to cooperate, President Roosevelt went to Casablanca, in Morocco; Quebec, in Canada; Cairo, in Egypt; Teheran, in Iran; the island of Malta, in the Mediterranean Sea; and Yalta, in the Soviet Union. He met with such world leaders as Chiang Kai-shek of China, Winston Churchill of England, and Josef Stalin of the Soviet Union.

*President Roosevelt's favorite dog, Fala, travels with him
on board a Navy ship in 1940.*

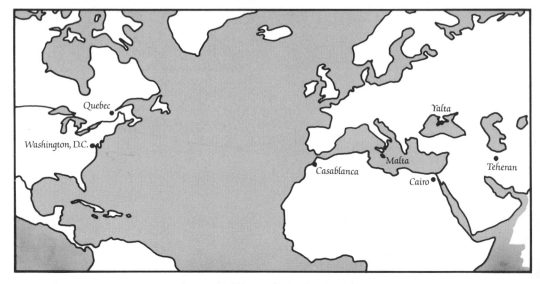

*To meet with other world leaders during the war, President
Roosevelt traveled to Casablanca, Quebec, Cairo,
Teheran, Malta, and Yalta.*

As commander-in-chief of the American forces,
President Roosevelt had to decide what would be
done, where it would be done, and when. He had to
coordinate American plans with those of the Allies.
The United States was at war on two fronts; it was
fighting in both Europe and Asia. Its men and ships
were fighting in the Atlantic and Pacific oceans.
Right after Pearl Harbor, the United States did not
have enough ships and planes to fight in both places
at once, so President Roosevelt had to make a hard
choice. He decided that the United States would
help Europe first.

In Europe, Germany attacked the Soviet Union. England and America helped the Soviet Union by bombing German factories night and day to stop them from making more war goods. Allied troops fought hard to rid North Africa of the Axis powers,

At the Cairo Conference in Egypt in 1943, President Roosevelt meets with Chiang Kai-shek, Winston Churchill, and Madame Chiang Kai-shek.

and then they landed in Italy. In June 1944, Allied troops finally landed in France. Although the Germans fought hard, the end of the war in Europe was in sight. Meanwhile, after early Japanese victories, the Americans stopped Japan at the battle of the Coral Sea and the battle of Midway Island in the Pacific. President Roosevelt had made his hard choices.

While President Roosevelt was meeting with other world leaders and deciding what was to be done, he also had to govern the American people. During wartime, he asked Americans to give up many of the things they wanted or needed. Each American was issued a ration book. The ration book contained coupons that limited the amount of food, clothing, or gasoline each person could buy. People could not always get meat, eggs, or butter in the stores. Even some clothing was hard to find. All those things were in short supply because the American armed forces needed them too.

Instead of cars, American factories made planes and tanks. Rubber went into tires, not balloons for the Macy's Thanksgiving Day Parade! Instead of nylon stockings, factories made nylon parachutes. But now there were plenty of jobs for Americans. As so many men were away at war, women learned to do their jobs. No one who could work had trouble finding work to do.

President Roosevelt also made an important secret decision. Scientists came to his office and told him that they thought they could make a very dangerous new weapon. He told them to go ahead and build the atomic bomb. He helped them get men, machines, and places to work. Very few Americans knew that this secret work was going on. In wartime, the President had to keep many secrets so that the Axis powers would not know what the Allies were going to do.

Being President during wartime also meant thinking ahead to peacetime. President Roosevelt had talked about four freedoms—freedom of speech, freedom of religion, freedom from want, and freedom from fear. The President wanted to build a world where everyone could have those freedoms. He wanted to keep the promises of the Atlantic Charter.

A UNITED NATIONS FOR PEACE

President Roosevelt knew that the Allies were going to win their war against the Axis powers. He was trying to win a peace that would last. That is why, in 1943, the governments of the United States, England, China, and the Soviet Union agreed to set up an international organization to keep the peace. These countries were known as the Big Four.

In 1944, the Big Four helped to start the United Nations Relief and Rehabilitation Administration, UNRRA. UNRRA was to work with the millions of people who needed food, clothing, and shelter. War had destroyed everything they had. The Big Four met again at Bretton Woods, New Hampshire. There they agreed to set up an international bank and an international fund to help nations rebuild when the war was over.

President Roosevelt told the American people that their country would join an international organization. He explained that this would not be a government to rule the world. Instead, the member nations would work together to prevent war. They would act together to keep the peace. After World War I, the United States had decided not to become a member of the League of Nations. This time, President Roosevelt wanted to make sure that his nation would cooperate with others.

Members of the Big Four governments met at Dumbarton Oaks in Washington, D.C., to make plans for a United Nations. They decided to have a General Assembly of all nations, no matter how big or small. There would also be a Security Council of big, powerful nations. In addition, the Big Four wanted to set up an international court and an economic and social council.

In 1945, when President Roosevelt met at Yalta with Churchill and Stalin, the leaders did not always agree. For a while, it looked as if the United Nations might be in trouble before it even began. By the end of the meeting, however, the leaders had resolved most of their differences. They decided to give the big countries a veto—the right to say no—if the United Nations wanted to do something any one of the big powers did not like. To do anything, the United Nations would need the agreement of the

In 1945, Winston Churchill, President Roosevelt, and Josef Stalin met at Yalta in the Soviet Union to discuss the war in Europe.

big, strong governments. The differences at Yalta proved that agreement would not always be easy to get.

Planning for a United Nations was difficult. Not all members were democracies. People spoke different languages, and they had different ideas about the ways nations should cooperate. President Roosevelt persuaded them to try. He helped nations prepare to join the United Nations, but he did not live long enough to see it become a reality.

6 President Roosevelt's Last Election

In 1944, F.D.R. faced another presidential election. The United States was still at war. The President did not think it was a good idea for a nation to change leaders at such a critical time, so he chose to run again. He was not feeling well, but he thought that it was important to stay in office until his job of winning the war was done. No other President had served his country four times, but the American people still wanted Roosevelt to be President. They gave him enough votes to defeat Republican governor Thomas E. Dewey of New York. President Roosevelt won by more than three million votes.

While he had been running for President, Mr. Roosevelt was busy with the war so he made few speeches. The Republicans were making lots of speeches. They attacked Roosevelt's politics. The President did make one famous speech against the Republicans. In this speech, he talked about his

At Hyde Park in 1941, President Roosevelt and Fala are visited by Ruthie Bie, the daughter of a neighbor.

Scottish terrier dog, Fala. Fala was the President's favorite pet.

> These Republican leaders have not been content with attacks on me, on my wife, or on my sons. No, not content with that, they now include my dog, Fala. Well, of course, I don't resent attacks, and my family doesn't resent attacks, but Fala does resent them. . . . He has not been the same dog since.

Of course, the President's dog did not understand politics, but people liked a President who would defend his dog.

After his reelection, President Roosevelt spent his time working to fight the war and win the peace. He traveled and he met with Congress. Then he left for his cottage in Warm Springs, Georgia. He needed a rest.

On April 12, 1945, the President died suddenly. It was a great shock to the American people. Back in Washington, six white horses waited for the train from Warm Springs. They drew a black-draped cais-

President and Mrs. Roosevelt in 1945, surrounded by their grandchildren.

son bearing the coffin to the White House. All along the way, people lined the streets to say good-bye to their President. Then Franklin Roosevelt was buried in the garden of his home at Hyde Park.

People all over the world sent messages to the Roosevelt family. Americans joined the Roosevelt family in mourning their great President. For some

Americans, President Roosevelt was the only President they had ever known. They remembered him with his cigarette and his broad smile, waving to them from a car. They remembered him talking to them on the radio.

Mrs. Roosevelt stayed on at Hyde Park. The President's dog Fala was with her. The nation went back to fighting the war and winning the peace.

THE NATION CARRIES ON ROOSEVELT'S WORK

When Franklin Delano Roosevelt died, Vice-President Harry S Truman became President. It happened so suddenly that he said, "I felt like the moon, the stars, and the planets had fallen on me." But he quickly learned to be President.

Within four months World War II was over, and soon the United Nations started to meet. President Truman gave the American people a "Fair Deal." In many ways, it was like the New Deal. Government would help Americans to go to school, to get good jobs, and to live better lives.

Congress passed the Twenty-second Amendment

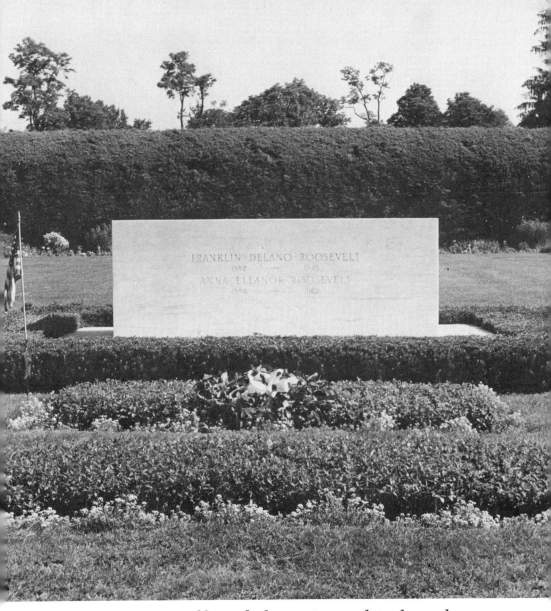

FRANKLIN DELANO ROOSEVELT
1882 ——— 1945
ANNA ELEANOR ROOSEVELT
1884 ——— 1962

*The graves of Franklin and Eleanor Roosevelt in the garden
at Hyde Park.*

to the Constitution. It said that no one could be President for more than ten years. Franklin Roosevelt had been elected President four times and had served for more than twelve years. Now he would be the only President in American history to win office four times.

He had done his job well. He had proved to the American people that government could help them during difficult times. He had showed them that government could help them to live better lives. He had led them during peace and through war.

In addition, President Roosevelt had taught the American people that a man could become President even if he was handicapped and could not walk without help. By his own example, he had proved to Americans that nothing is too difficult if you have hope and you try hard enough to succeed.

Index

Italics indicate illustration

93

About the Author

BARBARA SILBERDICK FEINBERG is a graduate of Wellesley College, where she was a Durant Scholar, Phi Beta Kappa, and won the Woodrow Wilson Prize for an essay on modern politics. After earning her M.A. and Ph.D. at Yale University, she taught political science on the college level. Her career as a writer began when she was a child and had an article published in *Jack and Jill* magazine. Since then she has had scholarly articles published and is now a free-lance writer and editor of college textbooks in the social sciences. She is married to Gerald Feinberg, an author and Chairman of the Department of Physics at Columbia University. They have two young sons and a Yorkshire terrier, and live in New York City.